A Very Small Book on K-1

A journey from reflection, to discovery, to revolution

Written by Warren Burda
Illustrated by Jeff Sheldon

A Very Small Book on K-12 Public Education First Edition, Paperback
Publication Date: December 2020
Publisher: Alpha Academic Press
ISBN: 978-1-948210-11-9

Alpha Academic Press

Published in the United States of America

Copyright © 2020

Introduction

I didn't plan to write a book, and my friend, Jeff, didn't plan on illustrating one, but we did. My writing isn't perfect and neither are his cartoon drawings, but they work well together. Mrs. Wandle, my fifth-grade teacher, taught me how to write a book introduction, but it would be 58 years till I actually did so. I hope I remember how to do it.

Teaching is what God called me to do. I did it faithfully for 44 years. During my career, I heard about, read about, and/or participated in numerous strategies and programs [e.g., Madeline Hunter, Cooperative Learning, appropriating more money, and No Child Left Behind] that were supposed to help us teachers become superstars and fix K-12 public education. Though generally well intentioned, these strategies and programs (often with high price tags) ultimately fail because they address only symptoms of the problem, not its cause; resulting in disengaged students and frustrated, unhappy teachers and school administrators. Many teachers leave the profession within their first five years; never to return. It is a national tragedy.

K-12 public education has been on this merry-go-round since the 1950's. After I retired, I decided to do something about it; hence this very small book with some very big revolutionary ideas about educational policy and reform. In 4,286 words in width and 68 pages in length (most of which are cartoon illustrated), the book achieves a first: it identifies the actual cause of the education tragedy, gives achievable remedies to fix it, and puts forth a simple action plan to incorporate the remedies into law and policy. When this is accomplished, K-12 public school instruction, learning, and teacher performance evaluation will be set free from that which binds them. Students, teachers, and school administrators will have their proper share of legislated power. Their voices will be fully heard.

The book's illustrator, Jeff Sheldon, and I have over 80 years of combined experience in K-12 public education (our credentials). We are not well known (not even close), but Thomas Paine wasn't well known when his pamphlet, *Common Sense*, was published. It helped start a needed revolution. Jeff and I hope our book does the same.

Warren Burda

iii

TABLE OF CONTENTS

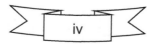

Dedication

This book is gratefully dedicated to the students of our public schools and to those who educate them.

Quote

If we get public education right, everything else will follow.

Steve Kagen

What This Book Was Founded On

This country was founded on revolutionary ideas.
So is this book.

Part I

The K-12 Years

Those of us who graduated from high school in 1971 remember valentine boxes, marbles, jacks, foursquare, hopscotch, and kickball.

We remember singing in grade school music programs, and then getting to go home early if our mom said yes.

We remember coloring within the lines, making pottery in art class, and dissecting worms in biology.

We remember playing school sports, wearing a letterman jacket, and cheering at school pep assemblies.

We remember passing notes in class.

We remember singing in choir and playing an instrument in band or orchestra.

We remember prom, strobe lights, live bands, study hall, and senior skip day.

We remember trying hard in some classes, and not so hard in others.

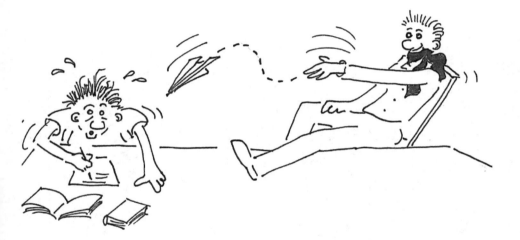

We remember participating in high school sit-ins to convince our administrators to allow girls to wear jeans at school.

We remember our high school graduation, but not the speeches.

None of us remember our report cards, unless our mom saved them for us.

Our K-12 education wasn't perfect; but nothing other than Jesus ever is.

Part II

Becoming a Super Star

I became a teacher in 1975.

I viewed the academy award winning short film, "Why Man Creates."

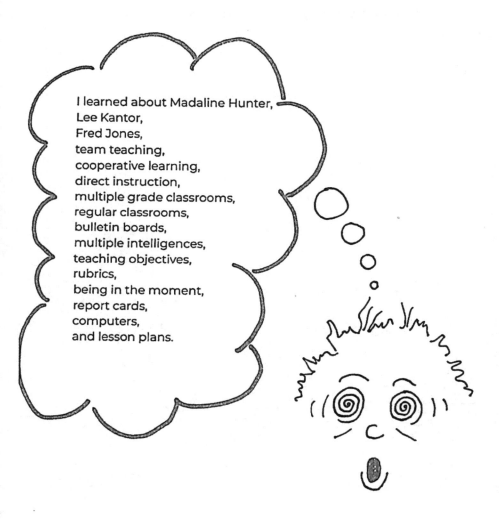

I learned about Madaline Hunter,
Lee Kantor,
Fred Jones,
team teaching,
cooperative learning,
direct instruction,
multiple grade classrooms,
regular classrooms,
bulletin boards,
multiple intelligences,
teaching objectives,
rubrics,
being in the moment,
report cards,
computers,
and lesson plans.

I attended countless faculty meetings, department meetings, and district meetings.

I went to state teaching workshops.

I was observed, evaluated, and debriefed.

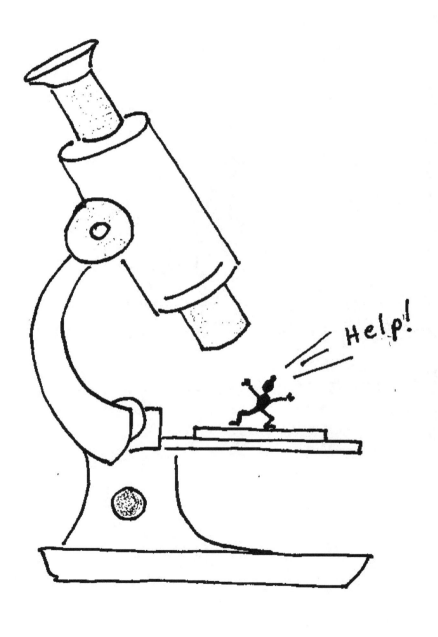

That's a **big** list.

With all that, I should have been an education super star.

Sometimes I was.

Sometimes I wasn't.

I wandered in the "Sometimes" wilderness for forty years.

Part III

Defining Moments / Realizations

It was 5:30 A.M.

My college graduation was a week ago.

I stood on the front deck of my fraternity house, leaning on a pillar.

God's Holy Spirit told me to do three things in my teaching career:

Show them that I love them.

Love them as I love you.

Feed my sheep.

So easy to write.

So hard to do.

Each year on a hot August day,
the school district holds its opening meeting.
All custodians,
cooks,
governing board members,
teachers,
administrators,
bus drivers,
nurses
meet together as one.
The faculty chorus sings.
Excitement and good will are in the air.
Coffee and donuts are provided.
The superintendent and governing board president
tell us what a great year we are going to have;
that we are family.
I always wondered what might have happened
if the family feeling had lasted
for more than one day.

The district asked for volunteers to help with a science textbook adoption.
I volunteered.
They put me on the committee.
Over a period of four-months we examined five textbooks as per district instructions; and then rated them 1-5, with 1 being our top choice.
We presented the results of our work to the assistant superintendent.
The district chose a textbook.
It wasn't among those on our list.

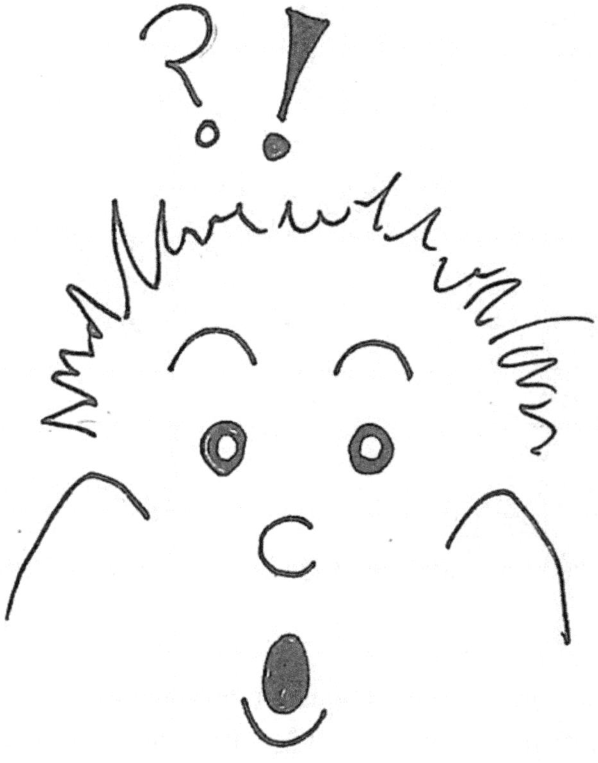

It was during a school board meeting.

I attended it because I was a school principal.

The board was considering cutting a music teacher and reducing a home economics teacher from full time to part time because of a loss in revenue due to a decrease in district enrollment.

To which I replied, "Just take away the junior high athletic program. That would fund the music teacher and keep the home economics teacher full time. Plus, the town will come up with the money needed to fund junior high athletics within the week."

The board voted to cut the teacher and reduce the other teacher to part time.

I left the district at the end of the school year.

It was after school.

I had returned to the district after four years as a principal.

I had three evaluations that year.

One was from the district.

During the post conference, my district evaluator told me that he had only taught one year and hated it.

To this I replied, "Then, why are you doing teacher evaluations for the district?"

My evaluator did not speak to me for a year.

I was prevented from transferring in-district to open high school government teaching positions.

I never told the evaluator that I got to teach government in another district and received a state award for excellence in teaching it.

Some things are better left unsaid.

It was a hot June Thursday afternoon.

One more day and the first week of summer school would be over.

My 25 students were repeating tenth grade English; so they weren't overly excited to be there.

I told them I was going to call home after school and tell their parents something good their son or daughter had done in class.

So I did.

I reached every student's parents except one.

Most of the parents told me that my call was the first time they could remember being told something their student had done well in school.

The next day, the girl whose parents I did not reach said, "If you call my dad at work during lunch today you will definitely get to talk to him."

Because of a simple phone call, my students were changed.

And not only them.

I became a better teacher and a better human being.

It was after school.

Two of us teachers and our administrator sat on a restaurant patio drinking a glass of wine.

We decided to start the first charter school in our city.

It had to be approved at a school board meeting.

During a coffee break at the meeting, the school district superintendent came and stood next to me.

The conversation was brief.

"Leading another insurrection Warren?" "Respectfully sir, when did I lead the first one?"

Years later, I considered his words to be the highest compliment he could have given.

My wife and I moved to another state.

My teaching certificate was not reciprocal in that state, or in any of the other forty-eight states if we had chosen to move there.

To become fully certified, I had to do the following things:

1. Order a probationary teaching certificate that allowed me to teach for two years.
2. Take and pass a state history course.
3. Attend and pass two English Structured Immersion workshops. (Both times I had to travel 110 miles each way and stay in a motel.)
4. Take and pass a subject test in government that made me highly qualified to teach it. (I thought my college degree was supposed to do that for me.)
5. Order a regular certificate.

The cost for all this was over a thousand dollars.

It was during a break from giving standardized tests at my high school.
I asked my seniors for their opinion about the tests.
This is what they told me.
"The tests are stupid."
"They make testing companies richer, and our district poorer."
"They don't make us better students."
"They aren't valid or relevant."
"They are a total waste of our time."
Fifty years ago we were saying the same thing.

A Remedy

It was 2015.

A vice principal and my five semester one government classes worked with me to create a high school teaching/learning framework that we all wanted to be a part of.

Forty straight government classes successfully implemented it up through my retirement in 2019, with very few changes made to the original framework.

During those four years, there was not one negative comment made about the teaching/learning framework on 960 end of class student evaluations.

It was the last final exam of my forty-four-year career.
My period 3 government students had a picture taken with me,
and we celebrated by eating small candy bars.
The bell rang, and the seniors headed out the door to graduation practice,
tossing their candy wrappers in the trash can.
Natalie was the last to leave.
She stopped in the doorway and said, "Thanks for being my favorite teacher."
Then, the door closed behind her.
I realized no more bells would ring for me, and perhaps for some of them too.
Some tears fell down my face as I bowed my head in prayer.
The students were gone, but their acts of Christlike faith, hope, and love-now treasures in Heaven-would remain.

Part IV

A National Tragedy

Most of the policies that govern K-12 instruction are made with little or no consideration of input from students, their teachers, and their school administrators.

Students have a voice but are rarely invited to speak at school board meetings; are rarely asked for their opinions by state and national legislators and are rarely invited by them to testify before a state or Congressional legislative committee on education.

Teachers have a voice, but if those in positions of power in district offices and on governing boards don't like what was said; teachers are often labeled as disloyal, denied positions applied for, or have their contract not renewed.

School administrators have a voice - the one given to them by the district.

The federal government dances around or blatantly ignores the Tenth
Amendment as it passes education laws telling states what to do.
The states pass laws telling school districts what to do.
The school districts tell their school administrators what to do.
The school administrators tell their teachers what to do.
And teachers tell their students what to do.
It is a national tragedy that those for whom we have public schools,
the students,
their teachers,
their school administrator(s),
have the least legislated power over it.

Part V

Fixing It

Remedy No. 1

We must get the legislatures of all fifty states to insert the following language in K-12 education certification law.

K-12 Teaching Certificate Reciprocity

1. A valid teaching certificate from one state is fully reciprocal in all other forty-nine states, with no added requirements or costs of any kind.

2. Application for renewal of a valid teaching certificate may be made to any state. The fee charged for renewal must be the same in all states. All state teaching certificates shall be renewed every five years for transcript evidence of having earned six college or university credits pertaining to teaching or subject area endorsements. The six college or university credits may be earned in any state. The colleges or universities granting the credits must be accredited. District in-service or education workshop credits do not count.

Remedy No. 2

We must get Congress to repeal federal law that continues standardized testing in our K-12 schools or get the courts to rule it null and void on the basis of the Tenth Amendment.

Remedy No. 3

We must get all state legislatures to insert the following language into K-12 education law. We must also get all public school districts to insert it into district policy.

K-12 Instruction

Part I

The power to create and make changes to a teaching/learning framework shall rest with the students, teachers, and administrator(s) of each public school.

They shall work together to create and implement a teaching/learning framework

1. that works for all of the school's grade levels and subjects taught.
2. that empowers the use of student gifts, talents, and learning styles.
3. that empowers the use of teacher gifts, talents, and teaching styles.
4. that empowers students to learn what is to be learned; and then use what is to be learned to create something, solve something, and/or respond to something.
5. that facilitates student presentations.
6. that facilitates student participation in assessment.
7. that accommodates IEPs.

Part II

Each school's teaching/learning framework must have governing board approval to be implemented.

During a specially called governing board meeting, a student, a teacher, and an administrator from each public school shall present their school's teaching/learning framework for initial approval or proposed deletions/editions to it after its initial approval.

The governing board and the presenting party shall engage in good faith discussion about what was presented.

Changes agreed to by both parties shall be made in the text of the teaching/learning framework by the clerk of the board at the meeting.

A vote is then taken. A simple majority is needed for approval.

Part III

Teacher performance evaluation shall be the sole responsibility of each state's public school district.

It shall not be based in any way on standardized test scores.

Each school district superintendent shall work with a teacher representative and an administrator from each school to create or make changes to a teacher performance evaluation based on the school's governing board approved teaching/learning framework.

A teacher performance evaluation and any proposed changes to it must have board approval before implementation.

Part IV

Each school's governing board approved teaching/learning framework and teacher performance evaluation shall be publicly accessible on the district website.

Part VI

A Teaching/Learning Template

A high school teaching/learning framework
for classrooms at school, at home, or online

(This template fits within remedy No. 3 of Part V.)

A quote from General Patton
(submitted by my teacher friend Natalie)

Don't tell people how to do things, tell them what to do and let them surprise you with their results.

1. The teacher flies a paper airplane (ours had "Portable 3 Airlines" written on the wings and "Hat, Hood, Beenie" written on the inside) as a reminder to students who forget to take off their hat, hood, or beenie. (The teacher needs to be sure the students are ready to catch it.) Each student gets to use two exemptions per quarter for a bad hair day. This management technique is fun and effective.

2. For most other things that need to be corrected by a student, the teacher uses a simple, but effective technique. In a voice that can only be heard by the intended student, the teacher asks, "Do you have the courage to _____ (example- not talk during a presentation?) If the student answers "Yes," the teacher walks away with the desired result and the student keeps their dignity. If the intended student answers "No" or "Not sure," the teacher says, "I'll be back in two minutes to ask the question again." This procedure is repeated until the student answers "Yes" to the question. (I never had to repeat the question more than twice.)

3. Brain research says that most students can fully pay attention for two minutes past their age before one or both hemispheres of their brain start becoming disengaged. Two simple techniques can effectively manage this. One is to place the right hand on the left shoulder and the left hand on the right shoulder. The other is a teacher-initiated school appropriate 30 second creative phone call interruption (that usually went something like this: "Sienna, your phone is ringing. This is Mr. Burda. How are things going for you in class right now?" "Pretty good." What is your team working on today?" "We're getting ready to present." "Good luck Sienna. I'll talk to you later." "Bye."

4. A team is composed of three to five students. Teams can easily be formed by counting off students 1-5, 1-4, or 1-3 for the number of teams that are needed. A team name is chosen by each team. Teams can be reformed as often as is desirable.

5. The teacher organizes what is to be learned into topics that can be taught in short periods of time by direct instruction. When teaching a topic, the teacher makes sure:

    a. that objectives are clear to the students.

    b. that concepts are explained and demonstrated in a variety of ways.

    c. that student understanding is checked.

    d. that objectives have been met.

The teacher prepares a review handout for each learning topic. For tracking purposes, each handout is given a number. Student understanding of each handout is assessed.

The teacher chooses the method or methods that can be used to answer each assessment item [i.e. choose the best answer; write it; talk about it; act it out; draw it; build it; demonstrate it, etc.]. Everything assessed is worth 1 point. The examples of topic handout assessment items show how we applied the 1-point value. Class time is provided for assessment preparation, but students may want to use out of class time for this as well. Assessments are given to students in one of three ways: individually, as a small group of 2-5 students, or as an entire class. Evaluation takes place immediately after an assessment or as soon as it is possible to do so. Evaluation must involve student participation. Each student's earned points are recorded. Assessments may be retaken if it is possible to do so.

Examples of Topic
Handout Assessment Items

Directions: Answer correctly to earn 1 point. Q: What free speech was most important to the Founding Fathers? Correct answer: political free speech.

Directions: List the six steps of CPR for an unconscious adult. Each step correctly listed earns 1 point. Each step listed in the right order earns 1 point. The correct steps in order are:

1. Call 911 or ask someone else to.
2. Lay the person on their back and open their airway.
3. Check for breathing. If they are not breathing, start CPR.
4. Perform 30 chest compressions.
5. Perform 2 rescue breaths.
6. Repeat until an ambulance or automated external defibrillator (AED) arrives.

Directions: Use the front and back of a 5 by 7 index card and the front of a second 5 by 7 index card to write a short fiction story about a topic of your choice. Use the back of the second index card to make a colored pencil illustration about something in the story. Give the story a title. Make sure you include all five elements of short fiction writing: setting, plot, characterization, point of view, and theme. Using a different color for each element, highlight where they are found in the story text. Conference with the teacher to determine earned points. The title earns 1 point. The illustration (with explanation) earns 1 point. Each of the five short fiction elements that is both present in the story and adequately developed earns 1 point. If the story action develops in a logical way and can be easily followed by the reader from beginning to end, it earns 1 point.

The Product

6. The Product is a team response that requires application of topic learning and the use of team member gifts and talents to create something, solve something, and/or respond to something.

For tracking purposes, each Product is given a number.

The teacher does the front end work - creating challenging Product prompts and initial Product tasks (teams can add tasks as needed). After that, other than the teacher helping teams overcome obstacles they face, it is the students' show. They are ones who work hard.

Teams divide up the Product work so each team member has a fair share to contribute to the Product. All team member Product contributions must be school appropriate. Teams track their work on a paper or electronic Team Product Chart - TPC. (We chose to use paper TPCs, which can be easily folded, placed in a plastic sheath, and stored in a box top marked Period 1, etc.) The TPC contains the following items: A heading at the top consisting of Team Name, Period No, A List of Team Members, and Product No; followed by three column headings (left to right): Column 1 - List of Product Task Work and Who Is Doing What For Each Thing Listed; Column 2 - In Process; Column 3 - Done (ready and able to be presented in class). Write Initial Product Organization Meeting and Product Presentation Meeting in column 1 for each Product. An X is used in column 2 to indicate when something listed in column 1 is in process and in column 3 to indicate when something listed in column 1 is done.

Teams decide to assign themselves work outside of class as needed to meet a presentation deadline. Each team member is responsible to have their work contribution ready and able to be presented when the team is called on to present a Product. Only work contributions that are part of a Product presentation quality for grading points.

A Product Review Meeting (attended by presenting team members and the teacher) is held immediately after a Product presentation. Additional Product Review Meetings are held for team members who are absent for a Product presentation. The Product Grading Rubric is used (as per the prompt) to determine the number of grade points earned individually by team members. Team members state the points they believe they earned in each category. For Category 2, team members tell what they did well and what they could have done better; then state the points they believed were earned. Everyone in attendance must agree with earned points chosen. The teacher has the final say if agreement is not reached. Presentation effectiveness is discussed, but not graded. Each team member's earned points are recorded.

Example of a Product Prompt

Our nation's health care system is broken. People wonder if members of Congress, who have excellent healthcare coverage provided for life, will set aside loyalty to party, special interests groups and stand together as one to reach agreement on a health care law that guarantees to all Americans the same health care that Congress enjoys. That's the public policy issue before your team. Make a 3-panel public policy portfolio on this issue; then use your portfolio to testify before the class. The portfolio is based on *Project Citizen*, a program developed by The Center for Civic Education. Each of our panels has two parts - Part A and Part B. The Product Grading Rubric will be used to determine individual earned grade points for Part A and Part B of each panel.

(Panel 1) The Problem
Part A: Identify the problem associated with the national health care issue. Explain it.
Include in your explanation each item below.
- Existing policies that deal with the problem (if there are any) and how effective each is
- The degree of seriousness and scope of the problem
- The levels of government (national, state, local) that are responsible for handling the problem and what they are doing about it
Part B: Use original graphs, photos, illustrations, and /or cartoons (so as to not violate copyright laws) to support your work in Part A.

(Panel 2) Possible Solutions
Part A: Research two possible public policy solutions to the problem. These are in addition to any existing policies. Explain the two possible public policy solutions. For each one, include detailed strengths and weaknesses and advantages and disadvantages for dealing with the problem. Choose which of the two possible public policy solutions is best able to address the problem and tell why your team chose it.

Part B: Use original graphs, photos, illustrations, and/or cartoons (so as to not violate copyright laws) to support your work in Part A.

(Panel 3) An Action Plan
Part A: Detail an action plan to implement the chosen policy solution from Panel 2. Include estimated implementation costs and a timeline for implementation.
Part B: Use original graphs, photos, illustrations, and/or cartoons (so as to not violate copyright laws) to support your work in Part A.

Product Grading Rubric

Category 1
My Task Work Contribution
(Things out of a student's control are taken into consideration.)

Which statement is true?	Earned Points
I contributed a fair share.	2
I contributed less than a fair share.	1
No work contributed	0

Category 2
Quality of My Task Work Contribution

Which statement is true?	Earned Points
All of it was done well.	3
Most of it was done well.	2
Not much of it was done well.	1
Not evaluated	0

Part VII

Let it be said of us

This small book identifies the national tragedy in k-12 public education,
and gives remedies that will fix it.

There may be opposition to enacting them into law and policy,
and there may not be many of us who want to do it,
but it was the same in 1776.

Theirs was a revolution for independence from England.
Ours is a revolution for needed change in k-12 public education.
It was said of them -
that they repeatedly petitioned King George and Parliament:
asking for redress of their grievances,
and letting them know that they would not stop
until their petitions were granted or military victory was achieved.

Let it be said of us -
that we contacted our Congressional Representatives and Senators,
our state legislators, school board members, and district superintendents:
asking that the three remedies put forth in this book
be enacted into education law and policy,
and letting them know that we shall not stop asking until it is achieved.

And once it is achieved,
let it also be said of us
that we are ever vigilant to keep it.

Postscript

It's been several months since Jeff and I finished this book. We hope you enjoyed reading it and that the cartoon drawings helped remind you of the child that is in all of us.

K-12 public education marches on, finding its way through Covid-19 health requirements and the disappointment of sport seasons cut short or cancelled, concerts unperformed, and graduation ceremonies not held. Students, their teachers, and their school administrators doubtless feel cheated of what could have been, while still striving for the ideal-the ideal student, the ideal teacher, the ideal school administrator. I tried to be that student for 16 years, that teacher for 4o years, and that school administrator for 4 years. I learned that while striving for the ideal may be great in theory, it too often causes us students, teachers, and school administrators to think that the blessings of our daily reality at school and in the classroom are not enough; that we are not enough. It simply isn't true. The publisher of our book has given it the opportunity to be part of the discussion about education policy and reform. Jeff and I are grateful for that. We hope you choose to be part of the conversation.

CPSIA information can be obtained
at www.ICGtesting.com
Printed in the USA
LVHW080410040121
675640LV00028B/346